GLENCOE SPANISH 2

A bordo

Communication Activities Masters

Prepared by
Leslie Lumpkin

GLENCOE
McGraw-Hill

New York, New York   Columbus, Ohio   Mission Hills, California   Peoria, Illinois

Printed in the United States of America.

Send all inquiries to:
Glencoe/McGraw-Hill
15319 Chatsworth Street
P.O. Box 9609
Mission Hills, CA 91346–9609

ISBN 0-02-646081-5

1 2 3 4 5 6 7 8 9   BAW   99 98 97 96 95

COMMUNICATION ACTIVITIES MASTERS
CONTENIDO

Communication Activities Masters

UNA LLAMADA TELEFÓNICA

VOCABULARIO

Palabras 1

A **Una llamada internacional.** Your friend is visiting Cartagena, Colombia. She needs to make several international calls but she doesn't know how. Read the following instructions and explain to her the steps she has to take to make her phone calls.

PROCESO DE MARCAR EN EL SERVICIO DE DISCADO DIRECTO INTERNACIONAL DDI

Ejemplos:

COMUNICACIÓN CON ESTADOS UNIDOS

Si desea llamar al teléfono No. 4291965 en la ciudad de Los Ángeles, marque en su orden los siguientes dígitos:

Código Inter-nacional	Indicativo del país	Código de área	Teléfono local
90	1	213	4291965

COMUNICACIÓN CON VENEZUELA

Si desea llamar al teléfono Nº 5001111 en la ciudad de Caracas, marque en su orden los siguientes dígitos:

Código Inter-nacional	Indicativo del país	Código de área	Teléfono local
90	58	2	5001111

En Caracas hay teléfonos de 6 y 7 cifras, lo cual no cambia el procedimiento descrito anteriormente.

COMUNICACIÓN CON FRANCIA

Si desea llamar al número 46871234 en la ciudad de París, marque en su orden los siguientes dígitos:

Código Inter-nacional	Indicativo del país	Código de área	Teléfono local
90	33	1	46871234

_____

_____

_____

_____

_____

Nombre _____ Fecha _____

B **¿Cómo se dice?** Your friend in Spanish I is trying to figure out what the right word is for each definition below. Help him/her out by supplying an appropriate expression from the vocabulary.

Necesito el libro de números de teléfonos.
Necesitas la guía telefónica.

1. Quiero un teléfono sin cable.

   _____

2. Necesito un aparato para tomar mensajes.

   _____

3. Los números que tengo que marcar para llamar a otro país.

   _____

4. Un número de teléfono que no es correcto.

   _____

5. Prefiero llamar de un teléfono público con casita.

   _____

6. El teléfono suena con un sonido diferente.

   _____

7. Donde se introduce la moneda.

   _____

8. Son los botones del teléfono.

   _____

Palabras 2

C **¡Yo también!** Your friend Consuelo recounts the following about her relationship with her grandmother when she was little. Find a new word for the underlined words in order to comment on how you had a similar relationship with your own grandmother. Follow the model.

Consuelo
Yo <u>hablaba</u> mucho con mi abuela.

Tú
Yo también conversaba mucho con mi abuela.

1. Yo <u>llamaba</u> mucho a mi abuelita.

   _____

2. No <u>escribía respuestas</u> a sus cartas.

   _____

3. Yo <u>quería mucho</u> a mi abuelita.

   _____

4. <u>Mi casa estaba</u> muy cerca de la casa
   de mi abuelita.

   _____

5. Yo la veía siempre <u>animada</u>.

   _____

6. Cuando mi abuela me invitaba a su casa,
   yo siempre quería ir <u>inmediatamente</u>.

   _____

D **¡Cuánto quería a mi nieto!** Take the role of your own grandmother and write her memoirs. Include the following information: how much she loved you when you were little, how often she telephoned you, when you used to visit each other, where each of you lived, what kind of conversations you had with each other.

Fecha _____

_____

_____

_____

_____

_____

_____

_____

_____

_____

Fecha _____

_____

_____

_____

_____

_____

_____

_____

_____

_____

ESTRUCTURA

El imperfecto de los verbos en -ar

A ¿Jugabas y practicabas...? Using the verbs below write a paragraph telling some of the things that you used to do when you were a little kid. Use your imagination and exaggerate what you did.

jugar	comprar	montar	caminar	llamar
levantarse	visitar	tocar	cocinar	lavarse
practicar	estudiar	mirar	hablar	bailar

_____

_____

_____

_____

_____

_____

_____

_____

_____

_____

El imperfecto de los verbos en -er e -ir

B **¡Qué memoria!** How good is your memory? Write a journal entry for every day last week. Include sentences about the weather, your emotions, and your physical condition. Use the imperfect tense.

domingo Nevaba. Yo estaba enferma. Tenía catarro y me dolía la garganta. Solamente quería dormir.

lunes

_____

_____

martes

_____

_____

miércoles

_____

_____

jueves

_____

_____

viernes

_____

_____

sábado

_____

_____

domingo

_____

_____

El imperfecto de los verbos *ir* y *ser*

C **Los secretos de familia.** Tell where you and other members of your family used to go in the following stages of your life or circumstances. Follow the model.

mis padres/novios
Cuando mis padres eran novios, iban mucho al cine.

1. yo/estudiante de primaria

   _____

2. mi abuelos/más jóvenes

   _____

3. mi madre/estudiante de universidad

   _____

4. mi padre/estudiante de colegio

   _____

5. mi tía favorita/joven

   _____

Los usos del imperfecto

D **Mi querida abuela.** You found a letter written 100 years ago by one of your ancestors to one of her friends. Read it, then write a report on what you learned, using the imperfect tense.

MI QUERIDA ABUELA
Cuando mi abuela tenía diez y seis años, ella iba a...

Querida Emilia,

Tú sabes que todos los veranos mi familia y yo vamos a Rancho Luna a pasar unas semanas con mis tíos, Eugenio y Micaela. Me divierto mucho aquí. Hace calor y el sol brilla en el cielo. A veces hay nubes y llueve. Todas las mañanas voy a la playa a nadar con mi prima Cecilia (ella también tiene diez y seis años como yo) y mi primo Guille (él tiene seis años). Guille es muy simpático y divertido. Él aprende a nadar pero no le gustan las olas. Cuando Cecilia y yo nadamos, él juega en la arena. A las doce regresamos a casa a comer el almuerzo. Tía Micaela prepara comidas deliciosas — bistec con papas fritas y ensalada, tortilla de papas, y frijoles. Después de almorzar lavamos los platos y dormimos la siesta. Por la tarde damos un paseo por el parque. Hablamos con nuestros amigos y comemos helado. Por la noche vamos a comer a un restaurante o preparamos la comida en la casa. Después de comer escuchamos la radio o hablamos con los amigos.

DE COMPRAS

VOCABULARIO

Palabras 1

A **Estuviste en la pescadería, ¿verdad?** Guess where your friend made his/her purchase.

Estudiante 1: Tenían muchas variedades de manzanas.
Estudiante 2: *Estuviste en el mercado.*

1. Compré pan francés e italiano.

   _____

2. Empujé el carrito por todos los pasillos.

   _____

3. La carne es más cara pero de excelente calidad (*quality*).

   _____

4. Tienen de todo: comestibles, ropa, cosméticos, medicinas, hasta libros y revistas.

   _____

5. Compré dos langostas.

   _____

6. La vendedora me dio un descuento porque compré muchas cosas.

   _____

7. Allí encontré frutas muy exóticas.

   _____

8. ¡Compré un bizcocho de chocolate fabuloso!

   _____

Nombre _____ Fecha _____

B **¡Qué organizado(a) eres!** Make your shopping list by naming three or more items you plan to buy at each of the following shops.

panadería   carnicería   pescadería   verdulería   pastelería

_____ _____ _____ _____ _____

_____ _____ _____ _____ _____

_____ _____ _____ _____ _____

_____ _____ _____ _____ _____

_____ _____ _____ _____ _____

Palabras 2

C **Yo hago las compras.** It's your turn to do the grocery shopping. Write a list of all the food your family will need for the week. Be sure to include quantities for all items.

Nombre _____ Fecha _____

D **¿Cómo lo prefieres comprar?** Using the clues, write the type of containers or amounts in which you buy the following items.

Prefiero comprar un paquete de fresas congeladas.

1. jabón en polvo

_____
_____

2. jamón

_____
_____

3. atún

_____
_____

4. papas

_____
_____

5. arroz

_____
_____

6. camarones
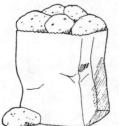

_____
_____

COMMUNICATION ACTIVITIES MASTERS
Copyright © Glencoe/McGraw-Hill

ESTRUCTURA

El imperfecto y el pretérito

A **El verano pasado.** Imagine you are writing a letter to a friend in which you tell him/her what you did last summer. Complete the following sentences.

Cada tarde *iba a la pastelería.*

1. Casi todos los días _____ .

2. Pero una vez _____ .

3. El 4 de julio _____ .

4. Siempre los domingos _____ .

5. De vez en cuando _____ .

6. El 15 de agosto _____ .

Dos acciones en la misma oración

B **La interrogación.** Imagine that you are a police officer interrogating a suspect about his/her whereabouts and activities at the time of a crime. Complete the following questions, then exchange workbooks with your partner and answer the questions.

¿Dónde estaba cuando *el crimen ocurrió?*
Estaba en la panadería porque tenía que comprar pan.

1. ¿Dónde estaba cuando _____?

_____

2. ¿Por qué no contestaste el teléfono cuando _____?

_____

3. ¿Qué hacías mientras _____?

_____

4. ¿Qué hiciste después que _____?

_____

5. ¿Quién salió del restaurante cuando _____?

_____

6. ¿Con quién hablabas cuando _____?

_____

Los verbos como querer y crecer en el pasado

C *¿Siempre, nunca o cuando?* Using the cues, tell whether you always or never felt that way when you were a child.

creer en
Siempre creía en Santa Claus.

1. creer en...

_____

2. pensar en ser...

_____

3. tener ganas de...

_____

4. poder tocar...

_____

5. preferir...

_____

6. saber...

_____

7. desear ser...

_____

8. querer vivir en...

_____

CAPÍTULO

3

EL CORREO

VOCABULARIO

Palabras 1

A **Aquí escribes la dirección.** You are teaching your younger sister how to address an envelope in Spanish. Using the drawing below, explain what you should write in the marked parts of the envelope.

Aquí escribes el nombre y la dirección del remitente.

1.

Doña Matilde Saldías
Sancho el Fuerte 10, 11°C
31007 Pamplona

5.

2.

Doña María Morrás

6.

3.

Alcalá 36, 1°drcha

4.

28009 Madrid

7.

1. _____

2. _____

3. _____

4. _____

5. _____

6. _____

7. _____

B **Ve al correo y...** Your Chilean friend is going to the post office for you. Write a note explaining three things you'd like him/her to do for you there.

> ## Querido(a) _____
> ## Quiero que... _____
>
> _____
> _____
> _____
> _____
> _____
> _____
> _____
> _____

Palabras 2

C **Un paquete.** Your friend is going to Chile next summer and wants to know how to mail a package back to the U.S. from a Chilean post office. Write a note telling him/her what is probably going to happen.

> *Entras en el correo y...* _____
>
> _____
> _____
> _____
> _____
> _____
> _____
> _____
> _____

COMMUNICATION ACTIVITIES MASTERS

Nombre _____ Fecha _____

D **En el correo.** You and your six year old cousin are at the post office. She asks you a lot of questions about the place. ¿How would you answer her questions?

1. ¿Qué hace esa persona detrás de la ventanilla?

   _____

2. ¿Por qué tiene que pesar el paquete?

   _____

3. ¿Qué son esas cajas pequeñas en la pared que tienen un número?

   _____

4. ¿Quiénes son esas personas que llevan una bolsa llena de cartas?

   _____

5. ¿Qué hacen con el correo?

   _____

6. ¿Por qué no hay entrega mañana?

   _____

ESTRUCTURA

El futuro de los verbos regulares.

A **¡Qué será, será!** Your job for the school yearbook is to predict what eight of your classmates will be and what they will do in the future.

David será médico y trabajará en un hospital en Nueva York.

1. _____
2. _____
3. _____
4. _____
5. _____
6. _____
7. _____
8. _____

El comparativo y el superlativo
Formas regulares

B **El mejor es...** An exchange student at your school wants to know what are the best in each of the following categories in the United States. Use the following adjectives to describe them: **interesante, grande, rico, famoso, importante, alto, popular.**

Los Ángeles es la ciudad más interesante de los Estados Unidos.

1. ciudad _____

_____

2. restaurante _____

_____

3. edificio _____

_____

4. teatro _____

_____

5. estado _____

_____

6. universidad _____

_____

7. parque nacional _____

_____

8. río _____

_____

CAPÍTULO
4

UN ACCIDENTE Y EL HOSPITAL

VOCABULARIO

Palabras 1

A **El pesimista.** Your friend phones you saying that the following things have happened. Respond by asking a question leading to a worst case scenario.

Me caí en la calle.
¿Se te rompió la pierna?

1. Me resbalé en el hielo.

_____

2. Anoche tuve un accidente en la bicicleta.

_____

3. Ayer por la mañana me hice daño.

_____

4. El sábado estuve en la sala de emergencia.

_____

5. Me caí en la escalera.

_____

6. Me lastimé en la clase de educación física.

_____

B **Los accidentes.** Interview a partner about any past accidents or injuries he/she may have had. First, write five questions you would like to ask your partner.

1. _____

2. _____

3. _____

4. _____

5. _____

Now, ask your partner the questions. Then summarize his/her answers below.

1. _____

2. _____

3. _____

4. _____

5. _____

Palabras 2

C **¿Qué pasó?** Using the illustrations below, write an article about what happened to Pablo López last week.

1.

2.

3.

4.

5.

6.

La semana pasada Pablo caminaba con su amiga Delia cuando...

_____

_____

_____

_____

_____

_____

_____

D **Las profesiones.** You are writing a brochure for Career Day about medical professions in Latin America. Write a brief description of the duties of the following medical personnel.

1. el/la cirujano(a) _____

   _____

2. el/la cirujano(a) ortopédico(a) _____

   _____

3. el/la anestesista _____

   _____

4. el/la enfermero(a) _____

   _____

5. el/la técnico(a) _____

   _____

6. el/la socorrista _____

   _____

ESTRUCTURA

El futuro de los verbos irregulares

A **Todo saldrá mal.** Your friend is clumsy and somewhat disorganized. She is going to do the following things. Say what you think will happen. Include the following verbs in your commentary: **tener, salir, venir, poner, saber, poder.**

Va a cortar carne.
No podrá cortarla y se cortará un dedo.

1. Va a patinar en hielo.

_____

2. Va a comer cinco pizzas.

_____

3. Va a comprar una bicicleta que tiene que ensamblar.

_____

4. Va a usar lentes de contacto después de llevar anteojos por 15 años.

_____

5. Va a pintar la casa de su abuela.

_____

Nombre _____ Fecha _____

El futuro de otros verbos irregulares

B **Los preparativos.** You and your classmates are preparing a surprise birthday party for your Spanish teacher. Using the illustrations below as cues, write questions about who will do the following tasks. Your partner will then suggest individuals for each job.

¿Quién podrá hablar con la directora?
Martina y Lorena podrán hablar con ellas.

1.

_____
_____
_____

2.

_____
_____
_____

3.

_____
_____
_____

4.

_____
_____
_____

El comparativo y el superlativo
Formas irregulares

C **Puede ser, pero...** Whenever you state an opinion about who or what is good, your friend quickly cites someone or something that is even better or worse. Write your opinion and then let your partner write his/her reply.

médicos

Estudiante 1: La doctora Matasanos es muy buena.
Estudiante 2: Puede ser, pero mi doctora es la mejor de la ciudad.

1. jugadores de fútbol americano

_____
_____

2. pizza

_____
_____

3. hospitales

_____
_____

4. películas

_____
_____

5. universidades

_____
_____

6. maestros

_____
_____

7. clases

_____
_____

EL COCHE Y LA GASOLINERA

VOCABULARIO

Palabras 1

A **El examen de conducir.** Your friend is helping you study for the driving exam. Tell him/her what you would do in each of the following situations.

1. Llegas a un cruce donde el semáforo (*traffic light*) no funciona.

   _____

2. Una llanta de tu coche tiene poco aire.

   _____

3. Quieres adelantar en la carretera.

   _____

4. Quieres doblar a la izquierda.

   _____

5. Estás conduciendo y oyes el sonido de una ambulancia.

   _____

6. Ves parado a un autobús escolar. Los niños están bajando del autobús.

   _____

B **El último modelo.** You are preparing a magazine ad to sell the car below. Include a title for the ad. Draw lines to and make comments about significant features. Mention the make and the price and include any other information you would use to market this car.

_____

_____

_____

_____

_____

_____

_____

_____

_____

_____

Nombre _____ Fecha _____

Palabras 2

C **Tengo que revisar todo.** You are going to drive your car 500 miles to the mountains next weekend. Write down all the things you need to do to prepare your car for the trip.

Tengo que verificar la...

_____

_____

_____

_____

_____

_____

_____

_____

_____

D **En la gasolinera.** You spent the whole afternoon at a gas station doing all the things you listed in Actividad C . The attendant was slow and kept making mistakes, like using the wrong motor oil, etc. Write a paragraph in your diary telling all the mishaps that occured at the gas station.

_____

_____

_____

_____

_____

_____

_____

_____

_____

ESTRUCTURA

El potencial o condicional
Formas regulares

A **¡No sería yo!** Read the following activities and think of people you know who wouldn't be caught dead doing these things. Then, state the alternative that the person would prefer.

conducir un coche de cambios
Jack nunca conduciría un coche de cambios. Preferiría caminar.

1. esquiar _____

_____

2. tocar el violín _____

_____

3. comer camarones _____

_____

4. vivir en un país extranjero _____

_____

5. comprar comidas congeladas _____

_____

6. estudiar griego (*Greek*) _____

_____

El potencial o condicional
Formas irregulares

B **Me podría decir...** Write down two requests you could make in each of the following places.

¿Me podría decir el precio del pan?

¿Podría decirme qué clase de pan es este?

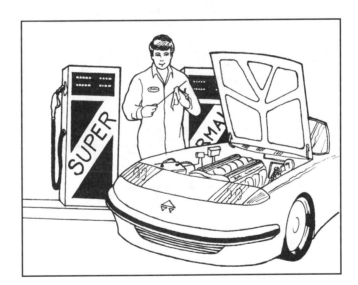

1. _____

_____

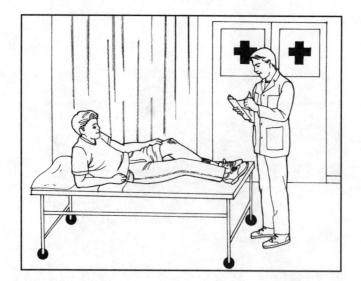

2. _____

3. _____

_____

4. _____

_____

C **A ver, ¿quién me los regaló?** How well do you remember who gave you certain things that you have? First list about ten gifts you have received in the past few years. Then, next to each item, state in a sentence who gave it/them to you.

las botas
Mi mamá me las regaló.

1. _____   _____

2. _____   _____

3. _____   _____

4. _____   _____

5. _____   _____

6. _____   _____

7. _____   _____

8. _____   _____

9. _____   _____

10. _____   _____

EL HOTEL

VOCABULARIO

Palabras 1

A **El Hotel Suecia.** You are in charge of choosing a hotel for the Spanish Club trip to Madrid. You have decided on the Hotel Suecia. Based on the hotel ad below, write a note to your Spanish teacher explaining the reasons for your choice.

HOTEL SUECIA
★★★★

EN PLENO CORAZON DE MADRID
LA UBICACIÓN IDEAL TANTO PARA NEGOCIO COMO PARA DIVERSIÓN, A UN PASO DEL MUSEO DEL PRADO, LAS CORTES, PUERTA DEL SOL, PARQUE DEL RETIRO, ETC.
128 HABITACIONES CON AIRE-ACONDICIONADO, BAÑO, TELÉFONO, TV. VIA SATELITE, MINI-BAR, CAJA FUERTE

SUECIA CLUB - EL HOTEL EJECUTIVO DENTRO DEL HOTEL
60 HABITACIONES NUEVAS EN UN ESTILO MODERNO Y ALEGRE CON TODO EL CONFORT QUE SE PUEDA DESEAR PARA UNA ESTANCIA AGRADABLE
SUITES EJECUTIVAS CON BAÑOS REDONDOS CON JACUZZI
HABITACIONES PARA NO FUMADORES

BAR TERRAZA
SALONES
SALA DE CONFERENCIAS

Marqués de Casa Riera, 4
28014 - MADRID
☎ **(91) 531-69 00**
FAX: 521 71 41 - Télex: 22313
HOTEL SUECIA
SU BIENESTAR EN MADRID

RESTAURANTE
Bolman
COCINA ESCANDINAVIA
"SMÖRGÁSBORD"
E INTERNACIONAL

El Hotel Suecia es muy cómodo...

_____

_____

_____

_____

_____

_____

_____

_____

_____

_____

B **¡Qué mala suerte!** Your vacation was marred by your experience at the hotel were you stayed. First, the receptionist couldn't find your reservations. Then, when he found them, he sent you to a single room, not a double as you wanted. There wasn't any bellman to carry your suitcases, so you had to carry them yourself. And, to make matters worse, the elevator wasn't functioning. Write about your troubles in a letter to your family, and include any other bits of rotten luck.

Palabras 2

C **Perdón, pero...** Call the receptionist to tell him/her your hotel room is in terrible condition. Then, let your partner play the role of the receptionist and write a solution to your problem.

La camarera no ha limpiado el cuarto.

Perdón, señor. Voy a mandar a la camarera a su cuarto en seguida.

1. _____

_____

_____

_____

2. _____
_____
_____
_____

3. _____
_____
_____
_____

4. _____

_____

_____

_____

D **Según el inspector...** You are the quality control inspector for a chain of hotels. Look at the room below and list what needs to be done to make it ready for a guest.

_____

_____

_____

_____

_____

_____

_____

_____

_____

_____

_____

ESTRUCTURA

El presente perfecto

A **Todavía no he...** Write a list of things you haven't done yet but that you hope to do someday. Then, ask your classmates if they have done what you want to do. Write down the name of the person who has already done it and tell the class. If no one has done it yet, tell the class *Nadie ha... todavía.*

Estudiante 1: No he comido tortilla española. ¿Has comido tortilla española?
Estudiante 2: Sí, la he comido. (No, no la he comido.)
Estudiante 1: No he comido tortilla española, pero... la ha comido.

1. _____

2. _____

3. _____

4. _____

5. _____

Los participios irregulares

B **Un menú estupendo.** Write down a menu that includes your favorite foods. Then, give a complete description of each dish.

Éste es mi famoso pastel. Lo he cubierto de chocolate. Y ésta es una ensalada que he hecho con pollo y frutas....

_____

_____

_____

_____

_____

_____

_____

_____

_____

Dos complementos con se

C **Un regalo.** You are looking for a birthday present for your mother. Tell whether or not you have given your mother each of the following.

perfume
Ya se lo he regalado.
No, todavía no se lo he regalado.

1. una cartera _____

_____

2. un suéter _____

_____

3. un cinturón _____

_____

4. unos guantes _____

_____

5. unas sandalias _____

_____

6. unos libros _____

_____

7. unas flores _____

_____

8. una blusa _____

_____

CAPÍTULO
7

A BORDO DEL AVIÓN

VOCABULARIO

Palabras 1

A **A bordo del avión.**

Estudiante 1

Compare the illustration (Dibujo 1) with the one your partner has. Working together, write five sentences describing the differences between the two pictures.

DIBUJO 1

Estudiante 1	Estudiante 2
1. Veo al piloto en la cabina de vuelo.	1. No veo al piloto en la cabina de vuelo.
2. _____	2. _____

3. _____   3. _____
4. _____   4. _____
5. _____   5. _____
6. _____   6. _____

DIBUJO 2

Estudiante 1

1. Veo al piloto en la cabina de vuelo.

2. _____

3. _____

4. _____

5. _____

6. _____

Estudiante 2

1. No veo al piloto en la cabina de vuelo.

2. _____

3. _____

4. _____

5. _____

6. _____

B **Atención señores pasajeros.** You are a flight attendant in a flight from Miami to Santiago, Chile. Write down the announcements usually made to the passengers during a flight.

Señores pasajeros. En estos momentos estamos volando por encima de los Andes y...

_____

_____

_____

_____

_____

_____

_____

_____

_____

Palabras 2

C **¡Qué aeropuerto!** You are the marketing manager for your city's new international airport. You have to prepare a promotional pamphlet that includes the following: number of runways, location of control tower, size of airport, type of planes that can land and take off, shops and restaurants it has, etc.

Aeropuerto Internacional El Eje. El único aeropuerto con las tiendas más exclusivas de la ciudad...

_____

_____

_____

_____

_____

_____

_____

_____

_____

D **Tienes que verlo, Mamá.** From your seat next to the window in the airplane you can see a beautiful view. Your mother, who is sitting next to you, is afraid to look out the window. Describe the landscape to her in detail.

Hay un pequeño lago con dos barquitos y...

_____

_____

_____

_____

_____

_____

_____

_____

Nombre _____ Fecha _____

ESTRUCTURA

Los tiempos progresivos

A **Yo estaba escribiendo, ¿y tú?** Write down what you were doing at the indicated times. Then, ask a classmate what he/she was doing at that same time and report to the class.

ayer a las siete de la mañana
Estudiante 1: ¿Qué estabas haciendo ayer a las siete de la mañana?
Estudiante 2: Yo me estaba desayunando.
Estudiante 1: Yo también me estaba desayunando.
A la clase: Ayer a las siete de la mañana, Juan y yo nos estábamos desayunando.

	Estudiante 1	Estudiante 2
1. esta mañana a las siete	_____	_____
2. esta mañana a las ocho	_____	_____
3. anoche a las once	_____	_____
4. anteayer a las diez y media de la mañana	_____	_____
5. el primero de enero a la medianoche	_____	_____

La comparación de igualdad con adjetivos y adverbios

B **Igual pero no en todo.** Look at the following drawings and compare each one to someone or something that compares equally and unequally to each one.

El BMW es tan caro como el Mercedes Benz, pero no es tan buen carro.

1. _____
   _____
   _____

44 A BORDO CHAPTER 7

COMMUNICATION ACTIVITIES MASTERS
Copyright © Glencoe/McGraw-Hill

2.

_____
_____
_____

3.

_____
_____
_____

4.

_____
_____
_____

5.

_____
_____
_____

La comparación de igualdad con sustantivos

C **Como los Pérez.** Using the following categories as clues, think of a person who has as many things as you do.

discos de
Tengo tantos discos de los Beatles como mi amiga Luisa.

1. revistas

   _____

2. zapatos

   _____

3. amigos

   _____

4. tarea

   _____

5. buenas notas

   _____

LA PELUQUERÍA

VOCABULARIO

Palabras 1

A **Muy observador(a).** How well can you remember the hair color and style of famous people? Write the name of a famous person in each of the following categories. Then, change workbooks with your partner and see if you can accurately describe each person's hair.

estrella de cine
Marilyn Monroe   *pelo rubio y un poco liso*

1. actor famoso _____

   _____

2. actriz de televisión _____

   _____

3. cantante _____

   _____

4. músico _____

   _____

5. reportero _____

   _____

B **El estilo.** How would you wear your hair in each of the following situations?

para visitar al presidente de los Estados Unidos
Quiero llevar el pelo en un moño, con flequillo.

1. para ir al colegio

   _____

2. para jugar al tenis

   _____

3. para ir a nadar

   _____

4. para ir a una fiesta de Halloween

   _____

5. para impresionar a un(a) chico(a)

   _____

6. para ir a un baile formal

   _____

Palabras 2

C **¡Qué peinados!** Look at the following hair styles and write what you think the hairdresser used to achieve that "look".

El/La peluquero(a) usó champú, rulos, horquillas y laca.

1.

_____

_____

_____

2.

_____

_____

_____

3.

_____

_____

_____

4.

_____

_____

_____

Nombre _____ Fecha _____

D **Una transformación.** You are a beauty consultant for a Spanish teen magazine that is sponsoring a beauty makeover contest. Look at the contest winner's picture below and write her a brief note telling her what you plan to have the hairdresser do to "transform" her.

Primero, la peluquera te va a dar un champú con un producto extraordinario...

_____
_____
_____
_____
_____
_____
_____
_____
_____
_____
_____
_____
_____

ESTRUCTURA

La colocación de los pronombres de complementos

A **La decoración.** You are decorating your room and need to get rid of several things. Ask your partner what to do with some of the items.

Estudiante 1: Tengo muchos libros. ¿A quién se los doy?
Estudiante 2: Pues, dáselos a la biblioteca pública, que los necesita.

1. revistas

2. diccionarios

3. discos de los Rolling Stones

4. sillas

5. televisión

6. balón para jugar vólibol

Acabar de *con el infinitivo*

B **¿Cómo? ¿No estás listo(a)?** Your friend has stopped by to pick you up for a meeting and you are not ready. State the things you have just done, that have caused you to be a little late.

Lo siento, pero acabo de ayudar a mi mamá a preparar la cena.

1. _____

2. _____

3. _____

4. _____

5. _____

6. _____

CAPÍTULO
9

LA COCINA

VOCABULARIO

Palabras 1

A **Los cocineros.** How does your mother or father prepare the following foods? State what condiment and method of preparation he/she uses.

1. la carne de res

_____

_____

2. las papas

_____

_____

3. las salchichas

_____

_____

4. las zanahorias

_____

_____

5. las chuletas de cerdo

_____

_____

6. el pollo

_____

_____

B **Para la comida.** Write down what ingredients you need to prepare each of the following. Then, tell your partner how you are going to prepare each item.

sopa de pollo	una comida baja en colesterol	sándwiches y ensalada de vegetales
_____	_____	_____
_____	_____	_____
_____	_____	_____
_____	_____	_____
_____	_____	_____
_____	_____	_____
_____	_____	_____
_____	_____	_____
_____	_____	_____
_____	_____	_____

Palabras 2

C **¿Se pelan o se cortan?** What do you need to do to the following foods before you cook or serve them?

Se pelan las bananas.

1.

_____

_____

2.

_____

_____

3.

_____

_____

4.

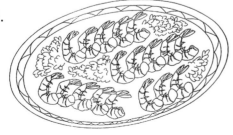

_____

_____

5.  _____
_____

6. 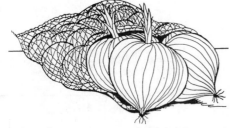 _____
_____

7. 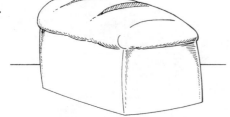 _____
_____

D **El restaurante Covadonga.** Your are planning the menu for your new restaurant and need to know which foods are the most popular. Take a survey of at least six classmates to find out which types of salads, soups, meat, poultry, fish and other seafood, drinks and desserts they want to see on your menu. Based on the survey, create a menu for your restaurant. Then, explain your menu to the class.

RESTAURANTE COVADONGA

Sopas	Ensaladas	Carnes	Aves
_____	_____	_____	_____
_____	_____	_____	_____
_____	_____	_____	_____
_____	_____	_____	_____
_____	_____	_____	_____
_____	_____	_____	_____

Pescados y Mariscos	Bebidas	Postres
_____	_____	_____
_____	_____	_____
_____	_____	_____
_____	_____	_____
_____	_____	_____
_____	_____	_____

Nombre _____ Fecha _____

ESTRUCTURA

El imperativo formal
Formas regulares

A Entre, salga, párese. What command do you hear in each of the following circumstances? Compare your answers with those of your partner. Tell the class which of your answers coincide.

¡No se mueva!

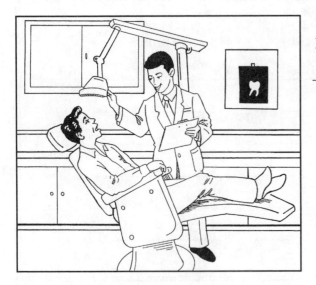

1. _____

_____

2. _____

_____

3. _____

_____

4. _____

_____

El imperativo formal
Formas irregulares

B ¡Hagan todo bien! Choosing from the verbs listed below, give a command to the person(s) below.

hacer   poner   salir   venir   decir   ir   ser   dar   conducir

1. Tu primo está jugando en el patio. Él tiene que almorzar.

_____

2. Tu hermano y tu hermana no han hecho las tareas.

_____

3. El conductor del taxi no es un buen conductor. Va muy rápido y no obedece las leyes del tránsito.

_____

4. La camarera quiere saber lo que Ud. quiere comer de postre.

_____

5. El perro ha entrado en la sala con un hueso (*bone*) en la boca.

_____

La voz pasiva con se

C **Los anuncios clasificados.** You work in the classified section of a Spanish newspaper and have to help the customers word the following ads in general terms.

un cliente quiere vender ropa de invierno muy barata
Se vende ropa de invierno a precios muy bajos.

1. un cliente quiere compartir un apartamento con otra persona

_____

2. un cliente necesita un profesor particular para aprender español

_____

3. un cliente quiere vender una mesa y dos sillas

_____

4. un cliente renta un dormitorio con baño

_____

COMMUNICATION ACTIVITIES MASTERS
Copyright © Glencoe/McGraw-Hill

CAPÍTULO
10

LA CARRETERA Y LAS DIRECCIONES

VOCABULARIO

Palabras 1

A **Lléveme al correos, por favor.** You have just arrived by train at your grandparents' hometown. You find a taxi with an inexperienced driver. Direct the taxi driver to the following places, starting each time from the train station.

Para ir al banco tiene que ir derecho por esta calle y después doblar a la derecha en la calle Tacón.

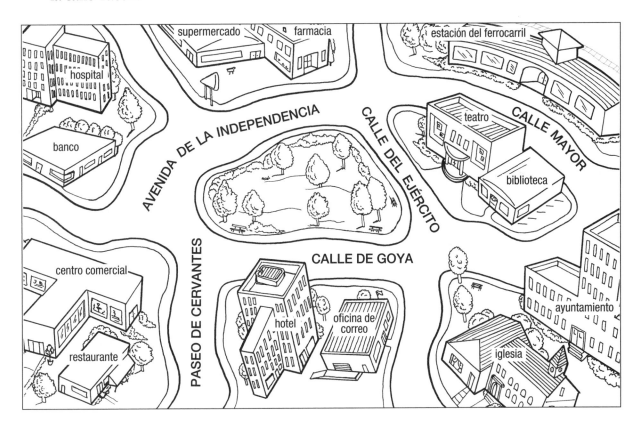

1. el banco

_____

_____

2. el supermercado

_____

_____

3. el correos

_____

_____

4. el centro comercial

_____

_____

5. el hospital

_____

_____

B **¿Dónde está...?** Write directions from your school to your favorite fast-food restaurant.
Then, read the directions to your partner who will make a map on a separate piece of paper
as he/she listens. Were your directions accurate and was your partner able to follow them?

Sales del colegio y doblas a la izquierda...

_____

_____

_____

_____

_____

_____

_____

Palabras 2

C **¡Qué tráfico!** Write a traffic report for your local TV station, indicating any ongoing problems, high-traffic areas, and rush hours.

Hay un embotellamiento (*traffic jam*) en la autopista. Un peatón tuvo un accidente en el cruce de peatones de la Calle Floridita y la Calle Argüelles...

_____
_____
_____
_____
_____
_____
_____
_____
_____
_____

D **¡Qué malos conductores!** You are preparing to take your driver's exam, which has made you hypersensitive to other people's bad driving habits. Make comments on the following things you witness as you drive with your driving instructor.

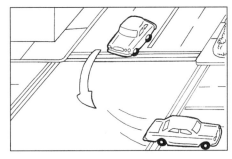

Ese conductor debe estar en el carril izquierdo para doblar a la izquierda.

1.  _____
_____

2. _____
   _____

3. _____
   _____

4. _____
   _____

5. _____
   _____

ESTRUCTURA

El imperativo familiar
Formas regulares

A **Unos consejos.** You are the parent of a teenager who has just received his/her license. Tell your child at least eight things he/she should always do when driving.

_____

_____

_____

_____

_____

_____

_____

_____

_____

_____

El imperativo de los verbos irregulares

B **Los mandatos.** Write the commands that your parents or someone else give in each of the following places. Give at least two commands.

en la casa
Haz la tarea.
Prepara la comida.

1. en la tienda _____

_____

2. en la playa _____

_____

3. en la clase de español _____

_____

4. en la biblioteca de la escuela _____

_____

5. en la gasolinera _____

_____

6. en tu dormitorio _____

_____

7. en el hotel _____

_____

8. en la peluquería _____

_____

9. en casa de un(a) amigo(a) _____

_____

10. en la consulta del médico _____

_____

El imperativo negativo

C **¡No, no y no!** What advice can you give a new student who has just enrolled in your school? Tell him/her what he/she can't do at school, what clothes not to wear, places he/she shouldn't go outside of school, food that he/she shouldn't eat in the cafeteria, and what he/she shouldn't do in class.

No corras en los pasillos (*halls*)...

_____

_____

_____

_____

_____

_____

_____

_____

_____

Nombre _____   Fecha _____

Los pronombres con el imperativo

D **¿Qué te dijeron?** What did your friends tell you when you told them the following? Use a command with a pronoun.

Ayer no te pude llamar porque llegué muy tarde del colegio y tenía mucha tarea. ¡Llámame hoy!

1. Estoy cansado(a). Anoche me acosté muy tarde.

   _____

2. Me duele la cabeza pero no quiero tomar ni aspirinas ni otras pastillas.

   _____

3. No puedo conducir porque no tengo licencia y me da miedo tomar el examen de conducir.

   _____

4. Tengo malas notas porque no escribí cuatro composiciones para la clase de inglés. El profesor me dijo que me daría otra oportunidad de escribirlas. No sé qué hacer.

   _____

5. No te quiero dar tus libros aunque sé que los necesitas para estudiar porque perdí los míos y me hacen falta para hacer las tareas.

   _____

CAPÍTULO
11

LOS BUENOS MODALES

VOCABULARIO

Palabras 1

A **¿Buenos o malos modales?** Pass judgment on the following children's manners according to their actions.

Juanito no habla cuando tiene la boca llena de comida.
Juanito es muy bien educado.

1. Margarita interrumpe a su mamá cuando ésta habla.

   _____

2. Joselito le dice secretos a Pepito en frente de los otros niños.

   _____

3. Cuando Maricarmen come, le da de comer comida de su plato al perro que está debajo de la mesa.

   _____

4. Pablito le abre la puerta a su maestra y se ofrece a lavar las pizarras.

   _____

5. Teresita nunca se olvida de decir "gracias" cuando recibe regalos.

   _____

6. Manolito habla mucho en el cine y tira mucha basura en el suelo.

   _____

7. Alvarito cuelga su ropa en el armario y deja su cuarto limpio.

   _____

8. Consuelito se pone la ropa de su hermana sin pedir permiso.

   _____

B **Los buenos modales.** You write a Spanish etiquette advice column. Look at the pictures and write what each person is doing wrong and tell what he/she should be doing instead.

No se debe comer con la boca abierta.
Se debe comer con la boca cerrada.

1.

_____

_____

2.

Perdone señora. ¿Me puede ayudar?

_____

_____

3.

_____

_____

4.

_____

_____

5.

_____

_____

Palabras 2

C **Una carta.** A Colombian friend who is coming to visit you wrote the following letter. Write a response.

> Querido(a) amigo(a),
>
> ¿Me puedes dar ejemplos de buenos modales en los Estados Unidos? Por ejemplo, ¿qué debo hacer para saludar a la gente y para despedirme? Si estoy con un grupo de amigos en un restaurante, ¿quién paga? ¿Y cómo me debo comportar cuando estoy sentada a la mesa? ¡Estoy un poco nerviosa!
>
> Saludos.
>
> Gina

> Querida Gina,

D **Las presentaciones.** The sentences below are scrambled. Find two complete introductions and write them in the correct speech bubbles under the correct picture.

No.
Igualmente, señorita.
Carolina, ¿conoces a Ricardo?
Me alegro de conocerlo, señor.
Buenos días.
Señorita Portela, le presento al señor Váldez.
Hola.
Carolina, Ricardo

ESTRUCTURA

El subjuntivo

A **¡Quieren que yo haga muchas cosas!** Your older brother wants you to help them plan your grandmother's eightieth birthday party. Make a list of all the things your brother wants you to do to get ready for the party.

Quiero que hagas la lista de invitados (*guests*) y compres los regalos...

_____

_____

_____

_____

_____

_____

_____

_____

El subjuntivo en cláusulas nomimales

B **¿Cuál es tu opinión?** Express one of your wishes, desires, hopes, or fears about each of the following.

Espero que no se sienten a mi lado.

1.

_____

_____

2.

_____

_____

3.

_____

_____

4.

_____

_____

5.

_____

_____

6.

_____

_____

El subjuntivo con expresiones impersonales

C **Mis consejos.** Your sister is just beginning high school. Make a list of things she must do to succeed. Use some fo the following expressions: *es necesario, es importante, es mejor, es posible,* etc.

Es importante que llegues a clase a tiempo.

_____

_____

_____

_____

_____

_____

_____

_____

_____

FIESTAS FAMILIARES

VOCABULARIO

Palabras 1

A **Una quinceañera.** Your pen pal Juan Antonio sent you this photo. Write back asking any questions you have about it.

Querido Juan Antonio, _____

_____

_____

_____

_____

_____

_____

_____

_____

_____

Saludos,

_____

B **Un bautizo.** You are a reporter for the society page of your local newspaper. Write an article about the baptism depicted below. Create the names of the persons involved, give details about where and when it took place, who attended, what people wore, where the celebration was held, and what food was served.

El primogénito de los Sres. Martínez fue bautizado...

_____

_____

_____

_____

_____

_____

_____

_____

_____

_____

Palabras 2

C **¡Qué fiesta!** Plan a Hanukkah or Christmas celebration. Answer the following questions, and include any other details you want.

1. ¿Qué fiesta vas a celebrar?

_____

2. ¿Qué vas a comer y beber?

_____

3. ¿A quién vas a invitar?

_____

4. ¿Dónde vas a celebrar la fiesta?

_____

5. ¿Vas a decorar tu casa? ¿Quién te va a ayudar?

_____

6. ¿Qué clase de música vas a tocar?

_____

7. ¿Cómo vas a celebrar la fiesta?

_____

D **Mi día de fiesta favorito es...** You are answering a letter from your Peruvian pen pal who asked you to describe your favorite family holiday. Tell him/her what the holiday is all about, and include a description of how you and your family celebrated this holiday last year.

Querido(a) _____ ,

_____

_____

_____

_____

_____

_____

_____

_____

ESTRUCTURA

El subjuntivo de los verbos de cambio radical

A **Ahora que soy el jefe quiero que tú...** Your mother has left you in charge of the household. Using the verbs below, tell other family members what you want or don't want them to do.

freír
Josefa, quiero que frías las papas inmediatamente.

1. dormir

_____

2. cerrar

_____

3. servir

_____

4. acostarse

_____

5. encontrar

_____

6. jugar

_____

7. perder

_____

8. seguir

_____

El subjuntivo con verbos como pedir y aconsejar

B **Vamos a Alaska.** You are the social director for a cruise ship that sails from Los Angeles to Alaska. Advise each of the the following passengers how they can have a good time and take advantage of all of the ship's activities.

Los pasajeros

Domitila y Tiburcio Pacheco / 80 años
Vicente Bonilla / 28 años / soltero
Magdalena Romo / 40 años / delgada
César Escobar / 30 años / enfermo
Amalia Batista / 55 años / fabulosa
Daniel Díaz / 9 años / muy activo
Claudia Acevedo / 27 años / profesora
    de una universidad
Javier y Amanda Aguilera / 45 años
Olguita Santamaría / 16 años

Las actividades

asistir a una conferencia sobre Alaska
leer una novela de misterio
hacer ejercicio en el gimnasio
ver películas extranjeras
bailar en una de las discotecas
quedarse en el camarote (*cabin*)
nadar en una de las piscinas jugar
    dominó o ajedrez (*chess*)
ir al baile de disfraces (*costume party*)
comer con el capitán del barco
correr

_____

_____

_____

_____

_____

_____

_____

_____

_____

_____

El subjuntivo con expresiones de duda

C **La máquina de tiempo.** You just came out of a time machine and stepped into the twenty-second century. You can't believe the many miraculous things you see. Using the expressions below, write eight sentences that you would include in your daily log.

no creer   dudar   no es cierto   no estoy seguro(a)   es dudoso

Es dudoso que una persona pueda hablar con otra persona usando un aparato que tiene el tamaño de un botón.

1. _____

2. _____

3. _____

4. _____

5. _____

6. _____

7. _____

8. _____

9. _____

10. _____

El subjuntivo con expresiones de emoción

D **Me alegro de que...** Complete the following phrases. Use your imagination.

Me alegro de que los marcianos (*Martians*) sean amistosos. Pero es una lástima que no sean verdes, que no coman queso y que no se comuniquen con las antenas que tienen en la cabeza.

1. Me alegro de... _____

_____

2. Julián está alegre... _____

_____

3. Están contentos... _____

_____

4. Estás triste... _____

_____

5. Sentimos... _____

_____

6. Es una lástima... _____

_____

7. Se sorprenden... _____

_____

LA NATURALEZA Y LA LIMPIEZA

VOCABULARIO

Palabras 1

A **Lo bueno y lo malo.** As an expert camper you can advise first-timers about the pros and cons of different camping equipment. Then, tell which one you prefer and why.

el hornillo / la hoguera de campamento (*campfire*)
El hornillo es fácil y rápido de usar, pero... Me gusta porque...

1. la tienda de campaña / la caravana / el albergue juvenil

_____

_____

_____

2. el saco para dormir / la hamaca

_____

_____

_____

3. el hornillo / la hoguera de campamento

_____

_____

_____

B **Un camping completo.** Look at the services offered by a campground in Spain. Make a list of everything the campground offers and tell which are important to you and why.

NUESTROS SERVICIOS

Contamos para su comodidad y servicio de: Oficina de Información, bar-restaurante, supermercado, peluquería, duchas de agua fría y caliente, piscina, autobús desde Valencia a la puerta del cámping, fregaderos, lavaderos, asistencia médica, vigilancia, custodia valores, recogida y entrega de correspondencia diaria, parque infantil.

• INFORMACION GENERAL: La estación de Ferrocarril, a 10.000 metros, gasolinera a 1 Km., talleres de reparación a 4 Km. y autobuses a 100 metros.

_____

_____

_____

_____

_____

_____

_____

_____

_____

_____

_____

_____

_____

_____

_____

_____

_____

_____

Palabras 2

C **La lavandería.** Your uncle has just opened a laundromat in a Hispanic community and wants you to write out the directions for using the machines in Spanish. Explain each of the following drawings.

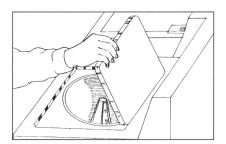

Primero, levante la tapa de la máquina.

1.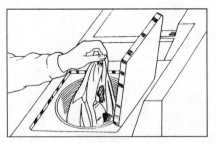

2.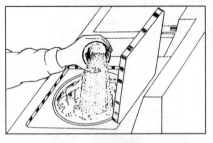

3.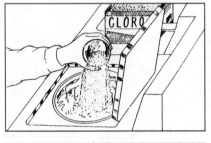

4.

5.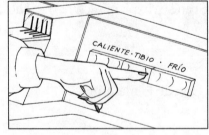

6.

D En la tintorería.

Estudiante 1

Compare the picture below (*Dibujo 1*) with the one your partner has. Working together, write five sentences describing the differences between the two pictures.

Dibujo 1

TINTORERÍA LA MODERNA
Tél. 245 20 27
Nombre *Luisa Rodríguez*   Sí ☐   No ☑
ALMIDÓN
031
PARA EL *Jueves 6*
PRECIO *300 P*

MIÉRCOLES 5

Estudiante 1	Estudiante 2
1. _____	1. _____
2. _____	2. _____
3. _____	3. _____
4. _____	4. _____
5. _____	5. _____
6. _____	6. _____

Estudiante 2

Compare the picture below (*Dibujo 2*) with the one your partner has. Working together, write five sentences describing the differences between the two pictures.

DIBUJO 2

Estudiante 1

1. _____
2. _____
3. _____
4. _____
5. _____
6. _____

Estudiante 2

1. _____
2. _____
3. _____
4. _____
5. _____
6. _____

ESTRUCTURA

El infinitivo o el subjuntivo

A **¡Quiero que él aprenda a cocinar!** Write five things that you want to do to improve yourself. Then, write five things that you want your friend to do to improve himself/herself.

Quiero comer menos papas fritas.
Quiero que Juan no coma pasteles.

ESTUDIANTE 1	ESTUDIANTE 2
1. _____	1. _____
2. _____	2. _____
3. _____	3. _____
4. _____	4. _____
5. _____	5. _____

CAPÍTULO 14

EL DINERO Y EL BANCO

VOCABULARIO

Palabras 1

A **La casa de cambio.** Your friend is going to Costa Rica. Write a note telling him/her what he/she needs to do to exchange money.

Primero busca una casa de cambio. Después...

_____

_____

_____

_____

_____

_____

_____

_____

_____

_____

B Un robo.

Estudiante 1

An American tourist who had just changed money at a casa de cambio was robbed. The police have just faxed you a copy of the exchange receipt. Your partner has also received a copy. Some of the information is unreadable. Ask your partner questions to fill in the missing information on your fax.

CASA DE CAMBIO TIBER, S.A. DE C.V.
SUC. REFORMA

TIBER
Casa de Cambio

DOMICILIO FISCAL
RIO TIBER No. 112 CUAUHTEMOC
06500 MEXICO, D.F.
TELS. 207-13-33 207-61-22

SUC. REFORMA
PASEO DE LA REFORMA No. 320 JUAREZ
06600 MEXICO, D.F.
TELS. 525-67-55 514-42-56

BOLETA-RECIBO
DE COMPRA
No. C 30638

COMPRA TRAVEL CHECK

MEXICO, D.F. A:
08/18

CLIENTE

Num. Ope. 47396

R.F.C. CCT-841108-KMA   AUT. SHCP-102-E-366-DESV-II-B-C-0451-27-01-1986   REG. IVA EXENTO 334880

SHCP

FOLIO
A 0070929

SECRETARIA DE HACIENDA
Y CREDITO PUBLICO

SUBSECRETARIA DE INGRESOS

CEDULA DE REGISTRO
FEDERAL DE CONTRIBUYENTES

CCT841108KMA
CLAVE DE REG. FED DE CONTRIBUYENTE

CASA DE CAMBIO TIBER,
NOMBRE

S.A. DE C.V.

1990

CANTIDAD	MONEDA	TIPO DE CAMBIO	IMPORTE EN MONEDA NACIONAL
$50.00	USD	N$ 3.07500	N$ 153.75 MN

INSTRUCCIONES:

EL CLIENTE MANIFIESTA BAJO PROTESTA DE DECIR VERDAD QUE RECURSOS
CON LOS QUE EL CLIENTE REALIZA ESTA OPERACION, NO PROVIENEN DE ALGUNA
ACTIVIDAD ILICITA, Y QUE ESTA OPERACION NO ES DE LAS QUE PROSCRIBE Y
SANCIONA EL ARTICULO 115 BIS DEL CODIGO FISCAL DE LA FEDERACION.

Francisco Rodríguez
RECIBI

COMERCIALIZADO POR: *PROVEEDORES DE FORMAS Y SERVICIOS, S.A. DE C.V.*
AV. CONTINENTES No. 80 VALLE DORADO TLALNEPANTLA, EDO. DE MEX.
R.F.C. PFS-850304-312 TEL. 379-18-49

LITHO FORMAS, S.A. DE C.V., R.F.C. LFO-540716-E-98
IMPRESOR AUTORIZADO EN EL DIARIO OFICIAL DE LA
FEDERACION, DEL 31 DE MARZO DE 1992.
TEL. 570-82-99

LA REPRODUCCION NO AUTORIZADA DE ESTE COMPROBANTE CONSTITUYE UN DELITO EN LOS TERMINOS DE LAS DISPOSICIONES FISCALES

Estudiante 2

An American tourist who had just changed money at a casa de cambio was robbed. The police have just faxed you a copy of the exchange receipt. Your partner has also received a copy. Some of the information is unreadable. Ask your partner questions to fill in the missing information on your fax.

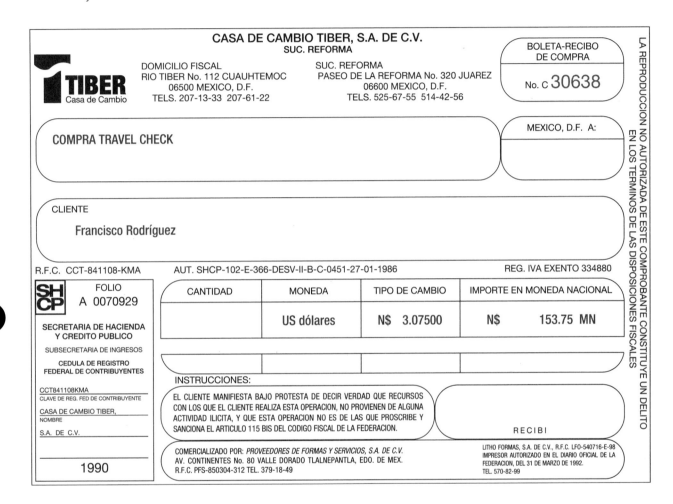

Palabras 2

C **¿Qué hacen?** You are a bank security officer watching a close-up video tape of people making normal transactions in a bank. Can you identify what these people are doing?

1.
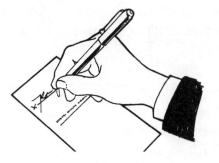
_____
_____

2.

_____
_____

3.

_____
_____

4.

_____
_____

5.
_____
_____

D **El banco.** What would you do in each of the following situations?

1. Ud. quiere pagar con cheques pero no tiene una cuenta corriente.

   _____

2. Gasta más dinero de lo que gana.

   _____

3. No quiere pagar con dinero en efectivo.

   _____

4. Quiere conciliar la cuenta.

   _____

5. Necesita pesetas pero sólo tiene dólares.

   _____

ESTRUCTURA

El imperfecto del subjuntivo

A **Un viaje.** You have just returned from a trip to Puerto Rico. Tell a friend what you had and didn't have to do before you left, and what advice your family gave you.

Fue necesario que comprara un boleto de ida y vuelta. Mi mamá me dijo que no era necesario que yo cambiara dinero...

_____

_____

_____

_____

_____

_____

_____

_____

_____

Usos del imperfecto del subjuntivo

B **El/La empleado(a) bancario(a).** Write down what a bank employee told a business class in high school that was opening a checking account.

Les aconsejó que hicieran un depósito antes de retirar dinero y...

_____

_____

_____

_____

_____

_____

_____

_____

Cláusulas con si

C **Los asistentes de vuelo.** Write down all the things you would do during a flight if you were a flight attendant.

Si yo fuera asistente de vuelo recogería las tarjetas de embarque y...

_____

_____

_____

_____

_____

_____

_____

_____

CAPÍTULO
15

AMIGOS, NOVIOS Y EL MATRIMONIO

VOCABULARIO

Palabras 1

A **El romance.** For a project in your sociology class, you are going to chronicle the romance and marriage of your grandparents. Include in your report where they met and how old they were, when their parents met, whether they went out with a group of friends or with a chaperon, how long their engagement was, and when and where they got married.

_____

_____

_____

_____

_____

_____

_____

_____

_____

B **La crónica social.** You are the social page editor of your local newspaper and have to write a column giving as many details as you can about the engagement party held at the home of Sr. Arturo Tamayo and Dra. Elena Aparicio de Tamayo in honor of their daughter, Elenita Tamayo Aparicio and her fiancé, Carlos de la Cueva Gutiérrez. Make sure you include how the engaged couple met, what the ring looks like, who was there, whether the couple's parents met for the first time, when and where the wedding will take place, educational background of the couple, etc.

_____

_____

_____

_____

_____

_____

_____

_____

_____

_____

_____

_____

Palabras 2

C **La boda de Lulú y Gabrielino.** You are a novice newscaster who covered the wedding of Latin America's best known and most popular movie couple, Lulú and Gabrielino. Look at the following illustration and write what you are going to read on the air. Be creative!

_____

_____

_____

_____

_____

_____

_____

_____

_____

D **Una boda.** Your pen pal Juan Jacinto sent you this photo. Write back asking any questions you have about it.

Querido Juan Jacinto,

_____

_____

_____

_____

_____

_____

_____

_____

_____

_____

_____

Saludos,

_____

ESTRUCTURA

El subjuntivo con cláusulas adverbiales

A **Yo por ti y tú por mi.** Tell your boyfriend/girlfriend what you will or would do, and what you expect from him/her in return. Use the following conjunctions in your sentences.

para que	de manera que	de modo que
con tal que	sin que	a menos que
No te dejaré nunca..		

No te dejaré nunca a menos que me dejes a mí.

1. Te diría todos mis secretos _____
   _____ .

2. Trataré de mostrar interés en tus pasatiempos favoritos _____
   _____ .

3. No te dejaré nunca _____
   _____ .

4. No hablaré mal de ti _____
   _____ .

5. Haría todo por ti _____
   _____ .

6. Guardaré tus secretos _____
   _____ .

7. Te ayudaría en todo _____
   _____ .

8. Seré tu mejor amigo(a) _____
   _____ .

El subjuntivo con *aunque*

B **Aunque todo no esté bien lo haré.** Based on the illustrations below, write what you will, won't, would, or wouldn't do even though... and invent some difficult circumstances.

Iré a las montañas con mis amigos aunque tenga que levantarme muy temprano.

1.

_____

_____

_____

2.

_____

_____

_____

3.

_____

_____

_____

4.

Pase sus vacaciones en la luna

Una adventura inolvidable

_____

_____

_____

5.

menú

ENSALADAS ....$ 15.00

SOPAS....................$ 10.00

SÁNDWICHES ....$ 25.00

CAFÉ ....$ 5.00

TÉ ....$ 5.00

POSTRES...............$ 20.00

_____

_____

_____

Nombre _____ Fecha _____

C **Buscaré el momento perfecto.** Using the adverbial time expressions below, state that you will do the following things.

cuando   en cuanto   tan pronto como   hasta que   después de que

organizar el garaje

Organizaré el garaje después de que termine mi tarea.
No organizaré el garaje hasta que mis hermanos saquen sus cosas de allí.

1. escribir una carta a mi prima

    _____

2. llamar a mis abuelos por teléfono

    _____

3. inscribirme para el SAT

    _____

4. estudiar para los exámenes finales

    _____

5. llamar a mi amigo en Alaska

    _____

6. casarme

    _____

7. comprar una casa

    _____

8. tener hijos

    _____

CAPÍTULO

16

LAS CARRERAS Y EL TRABAJO

VOCABULARIO

Palabras 1

A **Las profesiones.** Your class is writing a brochure for Career Day. Choose three professions and write a description of the qualifications, education, and personality traits someone would need for each.

Para ser ingeniero(a), se necesita entender las matemáticas muy bien y estudiar en una universidad. Los ingenieros deben ser pacientes e inteligentes.

1. _____

   _____

   _____

2. _____

   _____

   _____

3. _____

   _____

   _____

Nombre _____ Fecha _____

B **Sondeo: Las profesiones y los oficios.** Talk to your classmates to find one person who would like to do each of the following occupations. Write his/her name next to the occupation. Then, find out why he/she is interested in that occupation and write the reason in the third column.

Estudiante 1: Carmen, ¿te gustaría ser juez?
Estudiante 2: Sí.
Estudiante 1: ¿Por qué te gustaría ser juez?
Estudiante 2: Porque me gustaría trabajar en un tribunal.

NOMBRE	PROFESIÓN	RAZÓN
A Carmen le gustaría ser	juez	porque a ella...
_____	juez	_____
_____	ingeniero(a)	_____
_____	contable	_____
_____	escultor(a)	_____
_____	comerciante	_____
_____	piloto	_____
_____	abogado(a)	_____
_____	médico(a)	_____
_____	consejero(a)	_____

Nombre _____ Fecha _____

Palabras 2

C **Los consejos.** Your Cuban friend Manolo is looking for a job and wants your advice on how to proceed. In a brief note, outline the steps he should take to land a job.

Querido Manolo,

_____

_____

_____

_____

_____

_____

_____

_____

Saludos,

_____

D **El empleo ideal.** What's your idea of the perfect job? How many hours would you work? Where? For whom? What would your salary be? Write a paragraph about the "perfect job" in the space below.

_____

_____

_____

_____

_____

_____

ESTRUCTURA

El subjuntivo en cláusulas relativas

A **Buscamos a...** Your school is looking for candidates to fill the following positions. Students have been asked to write what some of the qualities of the ideal candidate would be. Write a job description using the subjunctive.

un(a) director(a)
Buscamos un(a) director(a) que sea bien organizado(a) y que sepa comunicarse bien con los alumnos y los profesores.

1. un(a) entrenador(a) para el equipo de fútbol _____
   _____
   _____

2. un(a) consejero(a) de orientación _____
   _____
   _____

3. un(a) enfermera(a) _____
   _____
   _____

4. un(a) profesor(a) de español _____
   _____
   _____

5. un(a) profesor(a) de música _____
   _____
   _____

Nombre _____ Fecha _____

El subjuntivo con ojalá, tal vez, quizá(s)

B **La cita.** You are supposed to meet your blind date at a museum. While getting ready you get nervous. Using *tal vez, quizás,* and *ojalá,* write down eight possible reasons why your date might not show up.

!Ojalá que no olvide nuestra cita!

1. _____

2. _____

3. _____

4. _____

5. _____

6. _____

NOTAS

NOTAS

NOTAS

NOTAS

116

NOTAS

NOTAS

118